STUDY GUIDE

Copyright © 2024 by Noreen Joseph

Published by Dream Releaser Publishing

All rights reserved. No portion of this book may be reproduced, stored in a retrieval system, or transmitted in any form or by any means—electronic, mechanical, photocopy, recording, scanning, or other—except for brief quotations in critical reviews or articles, without prior written permission of the author.

Unless otherwise noted, all Scripture quotations are taken from the Holy Bible, New Living Translation, © 1996, 2004, 2015 by Tyndale House Foundation. Used by permission of Tyndale House Publishers, Inc., Carol Stream, Illinois 60188. All rights reserved. | Scripture notations marked AMPC are taken from the Amplified Bible, Classic Edition, Copyright © 1954, 1958, 1962, 1964, 1965, 1987 by Lockman Foundation. | Scripture quotations marked NKJV are taken from the New King James Version®. Copyright © 1982 by Thomas Nelson. Used by permission. All rights reserved. | Scripture quotations marked TPT are from The Passion Translation®. Copyright © 2017, 2018 by Passion & Fire Ministries, Inc. Used by permission. All rights reserved. ThePassionTranslation.com.

For foreign and subsidiary rights, contact the author.

Cover design by Sara Young
Cover author photo by New Lynn Photos

ISBN: 978-1-962401-96-8   1 2 3 4 5 6 7 8 9 10

Printed in the United States of America

STUDY GUIDE

Noreen Joseph

DREAM RELEASER PUBLISHING

CONTENTS

Chapter 1. THE FAKE WORLD 6

Chapter 2. CAPTIVITY AND BROKENNESS 12

Chapter 3. RECURRING ADDICTION 18

Chapter 4. SPIRITUAL SENSES 24

Chapter 5. KINGDOM AUTHORITY 30

Chapter 6. ENCOUNTERING THE CREATOR GOD 34

Chapter 7. UNEXPECTED FRUITFULNESS 38

Chapter 8. NOW IS THE TIME 42

SEE
Through

Your Spiritual Senses

Noreen Joseph

Chapter 1

THE FAKE WORLD

> *In a "fake" world, there is no truth but deception. When we are unaware and do not have access to the real world, we are limited to the world of falsehood where everything looks real and good.*

READING TIME

As you read Chapter 1: "The Fake World" in *See Through*, review, reflect on, and respond to the text by answering the following questions.

REVIEW, REFLECT, AND RESPOND

What are the three major events in a human's life, and how do they relate to the chapter's theme of living in a "fake world"?

_____
_____
_____
_____
_____

What is the significance of Jesus choosing not to escape crucifixion, and how does it relate to His acknowledgment of belonging to another kingdom?

_____
_____
_____
_____
_____

How does the concept of the dragon's deception relate to the idea of living in a "fake world"?

_____
_____
_____
_____
_____

> *The nations were filled with wrath, but now the time of your wrath has come. It is time to judge the dead and reward your servants the prophets, as well as your holy people, and all who fear your name, from the least to the greatest. It is time to destroy all who have caused destruction on the earth*
>
> —Revelation 11:18

Consider the scripture above and answer the following questions:

What is the meaning of this verse, in your own words?

_____
_____
_____
_____
_____
_____
_____
_____

What role do spiritual senses play in distinguishing the real world from the fake world?

_____
_____
_____
_____
_____
_____
_____
_____

How does this chapter describe the relationship between materialism and the kingdom of the world?

What is the impact of deception on human behavior and beliefs?

How does this chapter depict the ongoing battle between the kingdom of darkness and the kingdom of light, and what role do we, as believers, play in this battle?

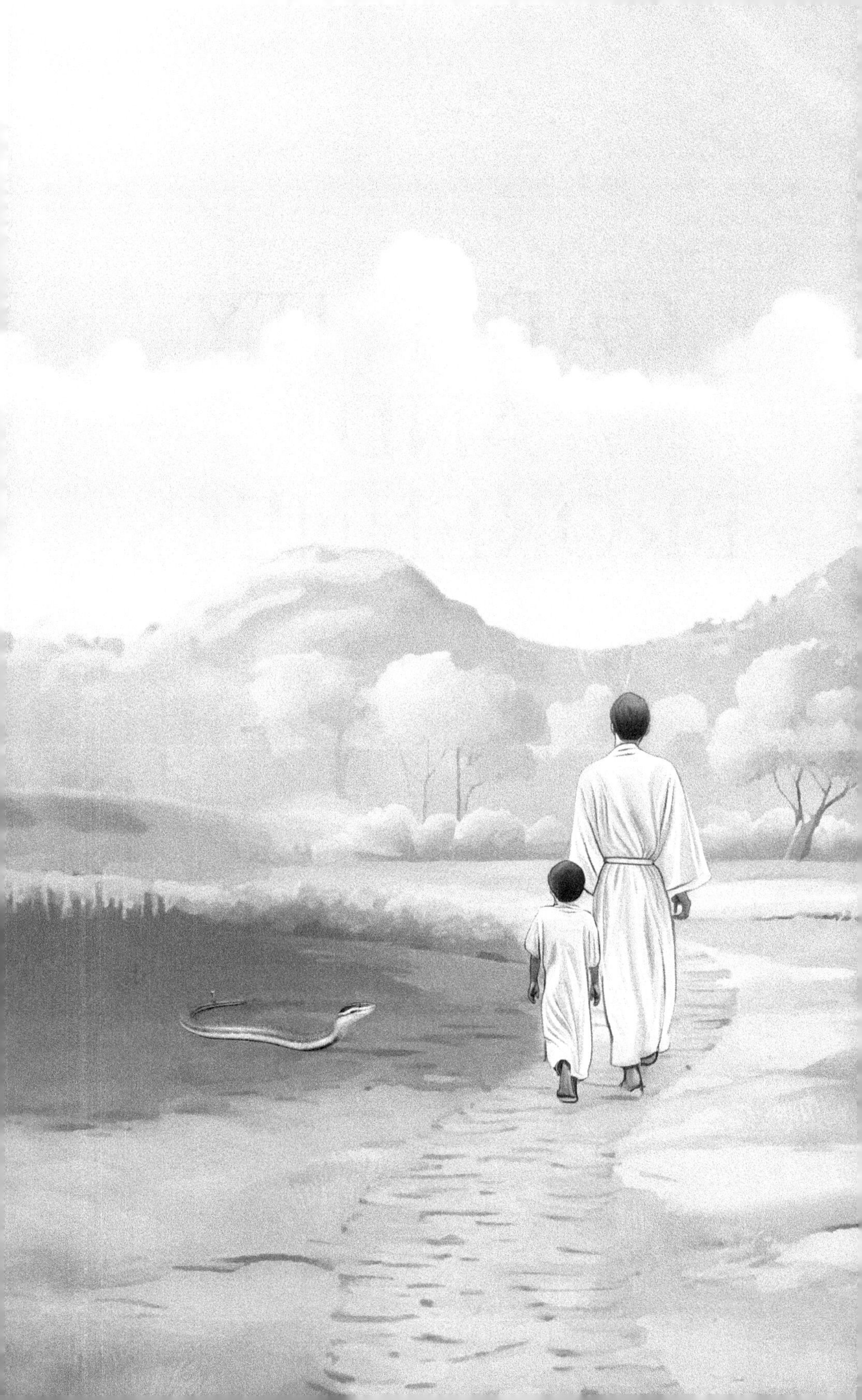

Chapter 2

CAPTIVITY AND BROKENNESS

When people are spiritually dead and disabled, evil spirits from the demonic realm have legal access to oppress them or possess their bodies.

READING TIME

As you read Chapter 2: "Captivity and Brokenness" in *See Through*, review, reflect on, and respond to the text by answering the following questions.

REVIEW, REFLECT, AND RESPOND

Reflect on how Adam and Eve's initial captivation by God shifted to being captivated by the world after disobeying Him. How does this concept of captivation relate to your own life experiences?

_____
_____
_____
_____
_____

Discuss the significance of having a "spiritual disability" inherited from Adam and Eve. How does this impact human behavior and relationship with God?

_____
_____
_____
_____
_____

In what ways can individuals ensure that God, rather than the world, captivates them? Provide practical steps or practices that can help maintain this focus.

_____
_____
_____
_____
_____

> *If My people who are called by My name will humble themselves, and pray and seek My face, and turn from their wicked ways, then I will hear from heaven, and will forgive their sin and heal their land.*
>
> —2 Chronicles 7:14 (NKJV)

Consider the scripture above and answer the following questions:

What stands out to you from this passage?

_____

_____

_____

_____

_____

_____

_____

_____

What would it look like for you to "humble" yourself before God?

_____

_____

_____

_____

_____

_____

_____

_____

How can praising and worshipping God or other spiritual practices help overcome personal struggles?

_____
_____
_____
_____
_____
_____
_____
_____
_____
_____
_____
_____

How can one balance material possessions and spiritual health in today's consumer-driven society?

_____
_____
_____
_____
_____
_____
_____
_____
_____
_____
_____
_____

Reflect on the concept of "spiritual captivity" and how it can manifest in various aspects of life, such as sickness or anxiety. How can one seek freedom from such captivity?

_____
_____
_____
_____
_____
_____
_____
_____
_____
_____

How does recognizing and breaking generational curses and unholy covenants contribute to spiritual freedom? Share examples or steps to achieve this in your own life.

_____
_____
_____
_____
_____
_____
_____
_____
_____
_____

How can experiencing brokenness from heaven lead to spiritual growth and alignment with God's purpose? Have you ever experienced this? Describe the situation.

_____
_____
_____
_____
_____
_____
_____
_____
_____
_____
_____
_____
_____

Chapter 3

RECURRING ADDICTION

> Human addiction is like a chronic disease that leads to a slow, painful death. It robs a human of his or her ability to respond to sin the way they have been created and purposed to respond.

READING TIME

As you read Chapter 3: "Recurring Addiction" in *See Through*, review, reflect on, and respond to the text by answering the following questions.

REVIEW, REFLECT, AND RESPOND

Define "addiction" in your own words.

_____
_____
_____
_____
_____
_____

Identify and discuss some common addictions. How do you think these addictions impact individuals and society as a whole?

_____
_____
_____
_____
_____
_____

How does addiction affect a person's relationship with the Holy Spirit?

_____
_____
_____
_____
_____
_____

> *Do not love this world nor the things it offers you, for when you love the world, you do not have the love of the Father in you. For the world offers only a craving for physical pleasure, a craving for everything we see, and pride in our achievements and possessions. These are not from the Father, but are from this world. And this world is fading away, along with everything that people crave. But anyone who does what pleases God will live forever.*
>
> —1 John 2:15-17

Consider the scripture above and answer the following questions:

What does this verse reveal about addiction?

_____
_____
_____
_____
_____
_____

According to this passage, why can one not love the world and the Father?

_____
_____
_____
_____
_____
_____
_____
_____

What strategies does the devil use to keep humans addicted, and how do these strategies play out in modern contexts?

What role can fasting play in overcoming addiction?

What is lust addiction, and what are its potential effects on individuals and their relationships?

_____
_____
_____
_____
_____
_____
_____
_____
_____
_____
_____
_____

Discuss how technology and the digital age contribute to the cycle of recurring addictions. What are some examples provided in the chapter?

_____
_____
_____
_____
_____
_____
_____
_____
_____
_____
_____

What solutions or strategies does the chapter propose for breaking free from recurring addictions? How have you utilized or how do you plan to utilize any of these strategies?

_____
_____
_____
_____
_____
_____
_____
_____
_____
_____
_____
_____
_____

Chapter 4

SPIRITUAL SENSES

The enemy's purpose is to defile and deceive every human being so that even the born-again Christian can remain spiritually inactive.

READING TIME

As you read Chapter 4: "Spiritual Senses" in *See Through*, review, reflect on, and respond to the text by answering the following questions.

REVIEW, REFLECT, AND RESPOND

How does the concept of spiritual death, as experienced by Adam and Eve, relate to the idea of spiritual disability in humans today?

_____
_____
_____
_____
_____
_____

In what ways do our spiritual senses serve as a lifeline in the kingdom of heaven, and how are they accessed?

_____
_____
_____
_____
_____
_____

Discuss the role of demonic spirits in influencing human behavior and how they contrast with the presence of the Holy Spirit.

_____
_____
_____
_____
_____

> *Shun immorality and all sexual looseness [flee from impurity in thought, word, or deed]. Any other sin which a man commits is one outside the body, but he who commits sexual immorality sins against his own body. Do you not know that your body is the temple (the very sanctuary) of the Holy Spirit Who lives within you, Whom you have received [as a Gift] from God? You are not your own.*
>
> —1 Corinthians 6:18-19 (AMPC)

Consider the scripture above and answer the following questions:

Does the perspective of your body being a temple help you shun sin? Explain your answer.

_____
_____
_____
_____
_____
_____
_____
_____

What does this verse mean when it says: "You are not your own"?

_____
_____
_____
_____
_____
_____
_____
_____

How can children be spiritually affected by the objects and media they interact with?

_____
_____
_____
_____
_____
_____
_____
_____
_____
_____
_____

What are some examples of how peer pressure and popularity can make children vulnerable to spiritual attacks?

_____
_____
_____
_____
_____
_____
_____
_____
_____
_____
_____

Describe the impact of fear on both physical and spiritual well-being, as outlined in this chapter.

_____
_____
_____
_____
_____
_____
_____
_____
_____
_____
_____
_____
_____

In what ways does spiritual warfare resemble a soccer game?

_____
_____
_____
_____
_____
_____
_____
_____
_____
_____
_____
_____
_____

What are the differences between physical and spiritual senses, and how do they interact in a believer's life?

How can the gift of tongues be used as a spiritual tool, and what is its significance in connecting with the kingdom of heaven?

Chapter 5

KINGDOM AUTHORITY

The authority and power of the Holy God was in His Son, Jesus Christ. Thus, we have access to the authority that Jesus had while He was on earth—the same authority that raised Jesus from the dead!

READING TIME

As you read Chapter 5: "Kingdom Authority" in *See Through*, review, reflect on, and respond to the text by answering the following questions.

REVIEW, REFLECT, AND RESPOND

How does Christ's sacrifice for our sins influence your understanding of forgiveness and redemption?

In what way(s) does believing in Jesus Christ empower you in your daily spiritual battles?

How does water baptism symbolize repentance and union with Christ in one's life?

> *Now faith brings our hopes into reality and becomes the foundation needed to acquire the things we long for. It is all the evidence required to prove what is still unseen.*
>
> —Hebrews 11:1, (TPT)

Consider the scripture above and answer the following questions:

What is the meaning and application of this verse in your own words?

_____
_____
_____
_____
_____
_____

How does understanding our completeness through union with Christ impact your daily decisions?

_____
_____
_____
_____
_____
_____

In what way does the testimony of faith and healing inspire you to trust in God's power?

_____
_____
_____
_____

How can you actively participate in spreading the gospel within your community?

How can letting go of unforgiveness help you experience spiritual victory and freedom?

Chapter 6

ENCOUNTERING THE CREATOR GOD

With the presence of the Holy Spirit inside us, we can grow our relationship with our Creator God and fellowship with the Trinity through the Holy Spirit, anytime and anywhere.

READING TIME

As you read Chapter 6: "Encountering the Creator God" in *See Through*, review, reflect on, and respond to the text by answering the following questions.

REVIEW, REFLECT, AND RESPOND

Describe the Trinity in your own words.

_____
_____
_____
_____
_____
_____
_____

How has encountering Jesus through the Word of God affected your life?

_____
_____
_____
_____
_____
_____
_____

In what ways does the presence of the Holy Spirit influence your interactions with others?

_____
_____
_____
_____
_____
_____

> *May the grace of the Lord Jesus Christ, the love of God, and the fellowship of the Holy Spirit be with you all.*
>
> —2 Corinthians 13:14

Consider the scripture above and answer the following questions:

What does this verse reveal about the nature of God?

_____
_____
_____
_____
_____
_____
_____
_____
_____

How can recognizing the Holy Spirit as a helper and advocate change your approach to challenges?

_____
_____
_____
_____
_____
_____
_____
_____
_____
_____

How does the concept of the Trinity help you understand your identity and purpose as a believer?

How does the concept of God as a Father figure influence your relationship with Him?

Chapter 7

UNEXPECTED FRUITFULNESS

The Lord works with those who are willing and available to work with Him.

READING TIME

As you read Chapter 7: "Unexpected Fruitfulness" in *See Through*, review, reflect on, and respond to the text by answering the following questions.

REVIEW, REFLECT, AND RESPOND

How does tithing reflect surrender to God and influence financial blessings? Do you practice tithing? Why or why not?

_____
_____
_____
_____
_____
_____

What principles are involved in fasting, and how can it aid in your relationship with God and spiritual growth?

_____
_____
_____
_____
_____
_____

Explain how obedience to the Holy Spirit can result in divine encounters and blessings.

_____
_____
_____
_____
_____
_____

> *Just as the body is dead without breath, so also faith is dead without good works.*
>
> —James 2:26

Consider the scripture above and answer the following questions:

How are good works related to faith and spiritual fruitfulness?

_____
_____
_____
_____
_____
_____
_____
_____
_____

In what ways does building a personal relationship with God lead to physical and spiritual fruitfulness? Have you experienced this in your own life?

_____
_____
_____
_____
_____
_____
_____
_____
_____

What principles are involved in expecting and experiencing unexpected physical and spiritual outcomes?

_____
_____
_____
_____
_____
_____
_____
_____
_____
_____
_____
_____
_____

How can recognizing and trusting in God's promises impact our physical and spiritual journeys?

_____
_____
_____
_____
_____
_____
_____
_____
_____
_____
_____
_____

Chapter 8

NOW IS THE TIME

It's time to be restored from your spiritual disabilities and stay active with your spiritual senses. Your victory is waiting for you. Wholeness is your portion!

READING TIME

As you read Chapter 8: "Now is the Time" in *See Through*, review, reflect on, and respond to the text by answering the following questions.

REVIEW, REFLECT, AND RESPOND

What is the significance of the Holy Spirit's guidance in physical and spiritual practices? Why is the Holy Spirit essential for understanding and navigating spiritual truths?

_____
_____
_____
_____
_____
_____
_____
_____
_____

How do the prophetic messages from Isaiah 24-26 contribute to the understanding of judgment and redemption? What are your key takeaways from these passages?

_____
_____
_____
_____
_____
_____
_____
_____
_____

> *Work at living in peace with everyone, and work at living a holy life, for those who are not holy will not see the Lord.*
>
> —Hebrews 12:14

Consider the scripture above and answer the following questions:

What does it mean and look like "living a holy life"?

_____
_____
_____
_____
_____
_____
_____
_____
_____

How can you apply this verse to your current season?

_____
_____
_____
_____
_____
_____
_____
_____
_____

How do Genesis 2:19 and 3:22 emphasize the importance of human choice in the physical and spiritual journey? What are the implications of this for understanding the conflict between divine and worldly kingdoms?

_____
_____
_____
_____
_____
_____
_____
_____
_____

Explain the concept of citizenship in heaven. How does this citizenship impact a believer's expectations and responsibilities?

_____
_____
_____
_____
_____
_____
_____
_____
_____

Break down the roles that are described in this chapter (overcomers, chain breakers, curse breakers, serpent crushers, dragon slayers, and dominion takers). How do these roles illustrate different aspects of spiritual warfare and victory?

_____
_____
_____
_____
_____
_____
_____
_____
_____
_____

Which role do you think you are called to take up? Are you ready for this spiritual war and what are you doing practically to get ready?

_____
_____
_____
_____
_____
_____
_____
_____
_____
_____
_____

Take time to look over the bucket list provided at the end of this chapter. What would you adapt to your bucket list and why?

Follow us at:

Facebook: noreenjoseph2023
Instagram: noreenjoseph2023
YouTube Channel: Holyspiritministries2024

Contact us at:

Holyspiritministries2024@gmail.com

Noreen Joseph is a fourth-generation Singaporean Christian. Holding an MBA, she found great satisfaction working as a Business Broker prior to a near-death accident. After being radically rescued and through subsequent encounters with Jesus, her family continues to reap fruitfulness through her restored spiritual senses. A lifestyle evangelist, author, wife, and mother who lives with her family in Perth, Australia, Noreen is passionate about mentoring those who desire to be active in their spiritual senses.

Printed in the USA
CPSIA information can be obtained
at www.ICGtesting.com
LVHW020339101124
796164LV00011B/297